Can They Fix It?

Level 3 – Yellow

Helpful Hints for Reading at Home

The graphemes (written letters) and phonemes (units of sound) used throughout this series are aligned with Letters and Sounds. This offers a consistent approach to learning, whether reading at home or in the classroom.

HERE IS A LIST OF PHONEMES FOR THIS PHASE OF LEARNING. AN EXAMPLE OF THE PRONUNCIATION CAN BE FOUND IN BRACKETS.

Phase 3			
j (jug)	v (van)	w (wet)	x (fox)
y (yellow)	z (zoo)	zz (buzz)	qu (quick)
ch (chip)	sh (shop)	th (thin/then)	ng (ring)
ai (rain)	ee (feet)	igh (night)	oa (boat)
oo (boot/look)	ar (farm)	or (for)	ur (hurt)
ow (cow)	oi (coin)	ear (dear)	air (fair)
ure (sure)	er (corner)		

HERE ARE SOME WORDS WHICH YOUR CHILD MAY FIND TRICKY.

Phase 3 Tricky Words			
he	you	she	they
we	all	me	are
be	my	was	her

...nd is a Yellow level 3 book band.

Can you say this sound and draw it with your finger?

Can Sam fix the tux? It is a bad fit.

This is Sam. He can fix the tux.

Can Meg fix the fox cub? It is sick.

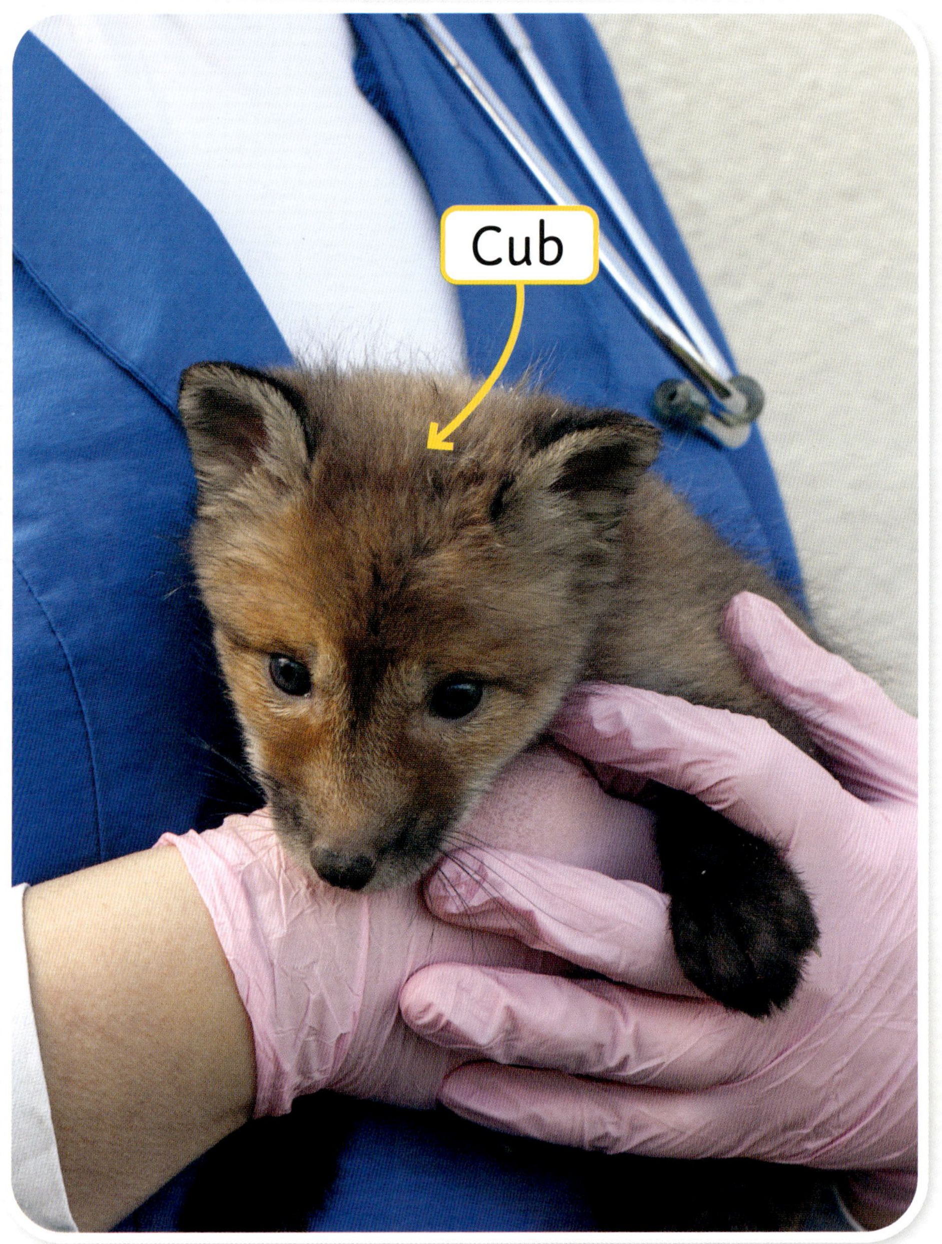

Meg can fix the fox cub.

Can Dex fix the box? The lid is not on.

Dex can fix the box. It has a lid.

Can Kat fix the bus? Pop! Hiss!

Kat can fix the bus.

©2023 **BookLife Publishing Ltd.**
King's Lynn, Norfolk PE30 4LS, UK

ISBN 978-1-80505-118-3

All rights reserved. Printed in China.
A catalogue record for this book is
available from the British Library.

Can They Fix It?
Written by Charis Mather
Designed by Jasmine Pointer

An Introduction to BookLife Readers...

Our Readers have been specifically created in line with the London Institute of Education's approach to book banding and are phonetically decodable and ordered to support each phase of Letters and Sounds.

Each book has been created to provide the best possible reading and learning experience. Our aim is to share our love of books with children, providing both emerging readers and prolific page-turners with beautiful books that are guaranteed to provoke interest and learning, regardless of ability.

BOOK BAND GRADED using the Institute of Education's approach to levelling.

PHONETICALLY DECODABLE supporting each phase of Letters and Sounds.

EXERCISES AND QUESTIONS to offer reinforcement and to ascertain comprehension.

CLEAR DESIGN to inspire and provoke engagement, providing the reader with clear visual representations of each non-fiction topic.

AUTHOR INSIGHT:
CHARIS MATHER

Charis Mather is a children's author at BookLife Publishing who has a love for reading and writing. Her studies in linguistics and experiences working with young readers have given her a knack for writing material that suits a range of ages and skill levels. Charis is passionate about producing books that emphasise the fun in reading and is convinced that no matter how much you already know, there is always something new to learn.

This book focuses on /x/ and is a Yellow level 3 book band.

Image Credits Images are courtesy of Shutterstock.com. With thanks to Getty Images, Thinkstock Photo and iStockphoto.
Cover – TimeImage Production, Eugene Zagatin, puruan. 4–5 – Stock Holm, Dragon Images. 6–7 – ALIAKSANDR PALCHEUSKI, Menno Schaefer. 8–9 – donatas1205, Roman Samborskyi. 10–11 – Andrius Kaziliunas, Roman Chazov

Lexile and AR levelled
PHONETICALLY DECODABLE
CERTIFIED LEXILE PARTNER
L&S
BASED ON LETTERS & SOUNDS
BookLife Readers
The Little Painter
By Shalini Vallepur
Flynn's Fantastic Flight
By A H Benjamin
Illustrated By Marcus Cutler
The Smell That Wasn't Funny
Illustrated By John Wall
FREE
ONLINE RESOURCES AVAILABLE
The Monster Cook Book
By Shalini Vallepur
Illustrated By Drue Rintoul
The Human Under My Bed
and
King for the Day
By Gunasekara
Illustrated By Irene Renon
Mum's Tum
By Graham Anthony
Illustrated By Batumashvili
BOOK-BANDED FICTION FROM LILAC TO LIME
FREE DOWNLOADABLE RESOURCES FOR EACH TITLE AVAILABLE ONLINE
Accelerated Reader

BookLife Readers

The BookLife Readers begin with the very basics of **phonetically decodable reading**. Starting with the earliest step of **CVC** words—words comprising of a consonant, a vowel and a consonant—and building on this combination slowly, the reader follows a prescribed format taken directly from the recognised **Letters and Sounds** educational document.

By aligning our books with Letters and Sounds, we offer our readers a consistent approach to learning, whether at home or in the classroom. Our Readers each feature a focus sound to help learners practice reading specific graphemes. These focus sounds will feature more heavily in that title than in others in the same band. The illustrations and photographs guide the reader, helping to deliver reading progression through the scheme in a colourful and exciting way. As a reader moves through the book band levels, the page numbers, levels of repetition and sentence structure complexity all advance at a rate which encourages development without halting enjoyment.

To find out more about this exciting reading scheme, visit www.booklife.co.uk

FREE
ONLINE
RESOURCE
AVAILABL

BookLife
Readers

Our BookLife Readers include activities,
quizzes and learning resources perfect
for the home or classroom environment.

Can you draw the focus sound
with your finger?

Hairy
Fairy Ears

HUNDRED
OF FREE
DOWNLOADA
RESOURCES

1.   Where do the fairies live?

2.   How did Azure's hairy e

3.   What did the witch w

(a)   Cut them off

(b)   Pull out the

(c)   Tickle them

What did Tessa

How would yo
change your

Can you make it through the maze to collect
the letter z? How many objects beginning
with z can you collect along the way?

Can you draw the focus sound
with your finger?

Can you draw the focus sound
with your finger?

BookLife
PUBLISHING